Parenting for School Success

Marcia Friedman

MWF Publishing

Library of Congress Control Number: 2011916328

ISBN: 978-0984016907

Printed in the USA

MWF Publishing
Dallas, GA

For information, please call 561-596.5280.

*This book is dedicated
to my husband and my children,
who respected my career choices.*

*A special thank you to
MWF Publishing
who went above and beyond
to see me through
this project.*

Introduction

Parenting is the term I use for any individual responsible for the physical, mental and emotional development of a child. It can be one of the most rewarding efforts for a human being. It can also provide some of the happiest and worrisome times in one's life. However, with practice and knowledge, success in parenting can be within a person's reach.

This book is going to focus on dealing with a child's school life. Although school usually starts with pre-school or kindergarten, a parent has to start preparing a child at birth. But I believe, if you missed that date, it is never too late to begin.

Parents have to know what the child is

experiencing at school. They need to know the emotional and scholastic triumphs and "tragedies" a student faces. A parent who is familiar with what is expected of a student at each grade and age level will be able to parent for school success.

Table of Contents

Chapter 1

Presenting Children For School Success

START EARLY

As I think about my years as an educator, I think about the involvement of parents.

1. More parents showed up for football games than "Back to School Night" after grade six. They know more about football.
2. Notices for academic programs for parent participation were less likely to be delivered than physical programs.

Why did the previous two statements stay with my thoughts? I believe some parents have poor school memories. School was not a wonderful place to be.

I believe if parents can change that feeling, their children will find learning (at school) an exciting opportunity.

I. How We Begin

Many parents become involved in the school through parent school associations, such as the PTA. They may work on bake sales, volunteer as aides on school trips, helpers in libraries, etc. These parents feel more at home in the school and may make their children feel more secure in the school setting.

Parenting for school success starts as soon as you know you are going to become a parent. However it is never too late to start.

- Health – get the best medical care you can while pregnant. Learn about good nutrition and exercise.

- Once your child arrives, provide your child with lots of language. Talk, talk, talk. Learn some nursery rhymes; recommendations will appear in the Appendix Parent Reference Books.
- Smile often and be dramatic. Your baby will respond to your body language.
- Imitation of your behavior and those around your child may likely be copied. Choose carefully the behaviors you wish to be copied.
- When reading to your child be responsive and project a love of reading.
- Provide toys that require active participation and creativity.

Age 2

The following abilities are to be achieved by age two:

LANGUAGE SKILLS

- Puts two words together "Mommy go" "Daddy see"
- Parents can understand simple needs that are spoken
- Uses some adjectives such as big, little, hot
- Has a vocabulary of about 50 words

SOCIAL SKILLS

» Wants to play with other children
» Can be separated from parents
» Uses "no"

Cognitive Skills

»   Can sort objects by shape and color
»   Scribbles
»   Understands out, up, down, on, in
»   Begins to play make believe

Physical skills

»   Walks alone
»   Begins to run
»   Can empty objects from a container

Age 3

At age three it is important for the child to have interacted with other children. Success in school has been believed by many educators to have a direct effect on a child's self-image. Self-image most usually is the response a child has from peers.

Many times, at age's three to five, we see how a child reacts to older people and don't see them in situations with their peers.

Watch your children at play with other children.

- Are they participating, or do they watch, or just ignore the action?
- Do they rule and others follow, or do

others quit?

- Will your children follow when it is not a good decision?
- When your child is not successful, what are his or her reactions?
- If you do not think the reaction is acceptable, change it.

The following abilities are to be achieved by age three:

LANGUAGE SKILLS

» Can say first name and age (usually puts up fingers)

» Uses pronouns (I, me, you, they) and some plurals (girls, boys, bikes, dolls)

» Answers simple questions (Is that your toy?)

» Identifies common objects

SOCIAL SKILLS

» Imitates parents and playmates

- » Takes turns
- » Is openly affectionate
- » No separation anxiety from parents

Cognitive Skills

- » Can copy a circle
- » Understands the concept of two
- » Plays make believe

Physical Skills

- » Can ride a tricycle
- » Walks up and down stairs
- » Builds a tower of more than six blocks
- » Can turn book pages one at a time

Age **4**

At age four many children are now in preschool. Social skills may be developing in different ways because exposure to different environments affects growth.

The following skills are to be achieved by age four:

LANGUAGE SKILLS

» Can describe the uses of common objects

» Speaks clearly

» Uses verb forms such as playing, walking, played, ran, told

» Tells stories

» Recites poems

SOCIAL SKILLS

» Cooperates with playmates

» Becomes more independent
» Tries to solve problems

COGNITIVE SKILLS

» Prints some letters
» Names some colors
» Draws a person with two to four body parts
» Understands same and different

PHYSICAL SKILLS

» Throws a ball overhand
» Kicks a ball forward
» Catches a bounced ball most of the time
» Dresses and undresses
» Uses scissors

Age **5**

Most children at age five will be entering kindergarten,

The following skills are to be achieved by age five.

LANGUAGE SKILLS

» Uses compound and complex sentences — Compound sentences are two or more short sentences connected by "and, or and but" — Jack has a horse and he rides it every day.

» Can say full name and address

» Uses future tense (will arrive, will know, will see)

» Can make up rhymes

SOCIAL SKILLS

» Wants to be like friends
» Wants to do things alone
» Follows rules

COGNITIVE SKILLS

» Can create imaginative stories
» Can identify four colors
» Can count ten objects
» Can distinguish between fantasy and reality
» Can copy a circle, a triangle, a square and a rectangle

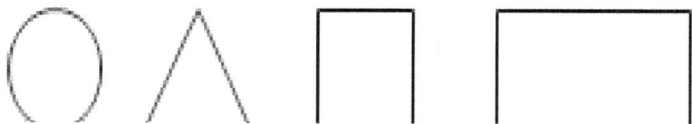

» Knows what is first and last

PHYSICAL SKILLS

» Hops, jumps, turns around.
» Takes care of personal needs (brushes teeth, bathes, combs hair)

Now your child is ready for school.

Teachers are human. They are supposed to understand your child and create a classroom that nurtures and expands your child's joy of learning. Teachers come with expectations and ideas of how to do this best. One thing I have learned through my years as a teacher and principal is: a child is successful when a teacher and parent understand that all children do not learn the same way.

STARTING SCHOOL

So now we come to the title of this chapter. "Presenting Children For School Success". You have now learned what skills your child needed to get to the door of kindergarten. Those are the first steps.

Now you are to present a child who looks like he or she is ready to learn. One who is not ready for the playground, but is ready for the schoolroom. A child who is clean, well-rested and well fed will do well.

I know it is difficult, especially if the caregiver(s) has to get to work and children off to school at the same time. Try to prepare as much the evening before as possible – so mornings are not hectic. Forms are helpful and here is a sugges-

Child: _____

	Clothes	Homework	Slips/Notes	Lunch	Extras
Monday					
Tuesday					
Wednesday					
Thursday					
Friday					

Form 1 - Child School Form

tion that you may want to copy.

Form 1

Check off each column and have a special place where everything can be grabbed on the way out in the morning. For the young children, you may even want a chart for bathing, brushing teeth, finishing breakfast. Small rewards can be given when all the necessary items have been completed without "nagging".

DRESS CODES

You are able to have more control over how your child presents his or herself at school in the lower grades. If the school uses uniforms, that makes it easy. If it does not, try to establish with your child what will be school clothes.

As your child enters the middle grades, they want more control over what they wear. Many schools have rules about

clothing, called a dress code. Be sure
you know what the code is.

I remember sending my daughter to
school in a skort outfit. It was as long as
a dress, and the only thing the store we
shopped had at the time. Dresses were
out, skorts were in. It took a while for
our school to catch up to new fashions.
They sent her home.

Another dress code situation was when
a very smart and popular student came
to school wearing two different color
socks. The socks were very trendy, and
the idea appeared in a magazine. I think
it was "Seventeen". Before long, there
were some followers. The dress code
had not had anything about socks. It
caused some disruptions. Have talks
about where they see themselves in the

work world. Wearing different arrangements of socks or something else "very different' may not be acceptable in the workplace.

In the high school years, conversations with your child can be difficult. Check the dress code before purchases are made. If you want changes in the dress code, find out who is in charge and go through the proper channels.

SELF IMAGE

At all ages, watch carefully to know who your child is with. Be aware of what he or she is doing. Listen for names and situations.

In the lower grades, it is a good idea to have a class directory. This would include students' names, addresses, and phone numbers. It only works while they are in contained classrooms. When they only have homerooms, and change classes, it becomes too cumbersome.

A good way to continue helping your child to grow, is to encourage participation in physical and/or artistic activities.

Some clubs that are helpful may be:
1. Debate club – to help "arguers" finesse their ability
2. Fashion club – to make students aware of how fashion can project their self-image
3. Drama club – great for students to use their imagination in being different personalities

If your school has a music program, and I hope they do, don't let peers turn your child away. I know a child who was very talented and because her friends thought music was for nerds, she quit. This had a strange effect on her social development. It took a long time for her to realize how capable and smart she was, and she didn't need to think that was a disadvantage.

At the high school level: Stop! Look! Listen!

Whenever you are having a conversation that may require change – think through what you want to say and gather all your information. Look at your child during the conversation. Watch body language and facial expressions. Keep the conversation calm, cool and collected. This is a conversation; so you want to hear what your child has to say – really listen.

In closing this chapter, listening to your child is another way of helping your child develop a self-image that will follow them for life. It should be adaptable and changeable. The student should know there are rules to be followed and lots of ways to build self-esteem.

Chapter 2
Using the School

Try to meet the teacher before your child does. Some schools have a "Meet the Teacher Night" prior to beginning a school year. If your school does not have this, see if you can make an appointment to meet the teacher early in the school year. This really helps you to understand situations between your child and the teacher.

Get a handle on what is expected of your child as far as special projects and homework.
- Are learning styles recognized?
- Is individualized instruction offered?
- Are project presentations to be student "only" or may families help?

- How are projects graded?
- How much homework will be given?
- How much time should be spent on assignments?

The questions I have introduced in the previous paragraphs should be asked as soon as the term starts. Prior to the term starting, you may be able to get a copy of the curriculum for your child's grade. If one is not available, the books that will be used will be helpful. If your child will be bringing books home, copy the Table of Contents and the Glossary. The glossary will be the vocabulary required for that grade. A student, who can define those words, will find understanding the subject matter a lot easier. It is really worth copying that list of words.

Vocabulary is a great part of any IQ test. Many times you can get an IQ score from just using the vocabulary section of an IQ test.

Years ago, I read about a study to see what leaders in government and corporations had in common. It was found to be their vocabularies. I have never seen any scientific proof of this conclusion, but it makes sense to me. If a high IQ on just the vocabulary section of an IQ test, is very much in line with the testee's IQ; then high IQ should equal the ability to understand whatever area they pursue and be able to rise to leadership.

If your child is having difficulty at school, find out what is available to solve the problem. Is the problem physical, social or academic?

Check if your child seems tired at school and at home. If he or she is not participating in physical activities. Has your child had a recent physical exam with a doctor? Make sure there is not a vision or hearing problem.

If the problem seems to be social, or academic; a talk with the teacher should follow a talk with your child.

A procedure to follow in solving problems is:
1. Hear your child's concerns
2. Go to the teacher
3. If not settled, go to the principal
4. If still not settled, go to the superintendent

Do not let a problem go unsolved. Most schools have people on the faculty who can help; if it is a learning disability, a health problem, a psychological problem or a social issue. A teacher will probably recommend whether your problem needs to be seen by some of these other faculty members. The area where many of these additional faculty members work is usually called Special Services.

It would be helpful to see a list of the complete faculty so you would have an idea of what is available to you.

Chapter 3
Dealing with Homework

By this time, I hope you have found out how much homework will be given and how it will be graded. You should also make sure that if the homework is not done in a timely manner or not done at all; you want to be notified.

I suggest a homework partner and or the availability of a homework hotline.

Provide a method for recording homework assignments if none is provided by the teacher. The recording should state subject and/or textbook, pages, objective (read pages, answer questions, write a summary, draw a picture, oral report, etc.) date assigned and due date.

Homework Assignments for:

Subject					
Textbook					
Objective					
Date Assigned					
Date Due					

Form 2 - Homework Assignments

The form on page 30 may be helpful to copy.

Now the student needs a place to do homework.

Learning styles need to be considered when choosing a homework site. I will acquaint you with information about learning styles so homework doesn't become a horrific time.

In the 70s, Dunn & Dunn, a husband and wife team, worked extensively on learning styles. They were on the faculty at St. John's University in New York State.

Dunn & Dunn focused on four areas: environmental, social, emotional and physical. Their thoughts were, if we met the needs of students in these areas, they could be more successful in school.

By talking to your child or observing them, you will find out where they work best. I am going to list the items, so you can check them off.

Physical
- ☐ Perceptual
    - ☐ Eyes
    - ☐ Ears
    - ☐ Hands
    - ☐ Body
- ☐ Needs food
- ☐ Works Best
    - ☐ Morning
    - ☐ Noon
    - ☐ Night
- ☐ Needs to sit
- ☐ Needs to move

Environmental
- ☐ Quiet/Noisy
- ☐ Bright/Dim
- ☐ Cool/Warm
- ☐ Formal/Informal setting

Social - to work with:
- ☐ Self
- ☐ Peers
- ☐ Pair
- ☐ Team
- ☐ Adult
- ☐ Others

Emotional – motivated by:
- ☐ Self
- ☐ Adult
- ☐ Teacher
- ☐ Persists
- ☐ Stops
- ☐ Responsible
- ☐ Structure
  - ☐ Needs structure
  - ☐ Long Range
  - ☐ Immediate

After you have taken a look at learning styles – choose a site and time when it is best to do homework. Think about lighting and whether music nearby would be a help or hindrance. Think about the temperature in the room and if your child can move around in the space.

Some materials to help are:
- Pencils, pens, markers, erasers, white out
- Paper appropriate for age level
- Dictionary, thesaurus, computer if available
- Library card

Teachers will usually suggest other materials. Look at the children's books and see what would be helpful.

Arithmetic at different levels would

mention – clocks, thermometers, rulers, yardsticks, compasses, calculators, scales, measuring cups.

Social studies offer a need for maps, an atlas, and possibly a globe. A good place to obtain materials is a travel agency. A student may plan a make believe, or maybe a real trip to a place being studied, and a travel agency can provide a wealth of information. A request for information to a state capitol or Chamber of Commerce is also helpful.

Science materials can usually be found in your pantry.

Unmotivated students may become excited about an assignment when they can feel or produce things. Arithmetic assignments are more real when they have measuring equipment. Social studies can be fun when someone out of school can share first-hand information.

HOMEWORK
RESEARCH

- Japanese students spend twice as much on homework as American students.
- US Department of Education report entitled What Works - *"Student achievement rises significantly when teachers regularly assign homework and students conscientiously do it."*

The report further states:

- *Average ability students who do three to five hours of homework a week usually get as good a grade as students of high ability who do no homework.*
- *Low ability students who do one to three hours of homework a week get as high a*

*grade as students of average avility who
do no homework.*

Time for Age Level

- Kindegarten through third grade
  20 minutes of homework per day
- Fourth through sixth grade
  20-40 minutes of homework per day
- Seventh and eighth grade
  60-90 minutes of homework per day
- High School
  90-120 minutes per day

Now that you are armed with how to
help your child be comfortable with his
or her homework, I hope homework will
be a pleasant time in your home.

Chapter 4
Skills That Help Learning

THINKING SKILLS
- Thinking skills are easy to see as you watch your child develop. First you see your child taking in the world around them. What you put in front of your child may become part of their personality.

OBSERVING is the first skill. Observation uses the senses of listening, touching, smelling, and not only seeing.

IDENTIFYING is the next thinking skill that is usually early to see. A child will say mama or daddy. This skill builds a vocabulary. It also is a big part of development of other skills.

- **COMPARING** is a skill that is used often in your everyday life. It is the ability to see how things are alike and different.

- The next thinking skill to be developed is **CLASSIFYING**. This means placing items into related groups. You may need to put things in alphabetical order, or from little to big.

- **IMAGINING** may result in inventing new ideas. Movies, autos, music – entertaining and necessary needs: many come from someone's imagination.

- **HYPOTHESIZING** – As one becomes more skillful in the previous skills, it is possible for them to come up with a solution to an unsolved situation. You may come up with several hypotheses. When the oil spill in 2010 took place, many suggestions were made on how to cap the oil that flowed into the Gulf of Mexico. Hypothesizing was used at this time.

- **CRITICIZING** becomes more skillful when many skills are developed. It is often used before the skills are developed. Then it is usually based on just like or dislike. A good criticism is weighted with good reasons and facts.

Other thinking skills that should be developed:
- Being able to detect true or false
- Being able to know what information is important and what is not

The **PAPER FOLD SKILL** helps to study for tests in science and social studies. Think about what the information for the test was about. Main ideas come into play. Example for a social studies test:

Happenings	Dates	People	Place
Wants to find new lands	1490s	Columbus	Spain
Asks for financial help		Queen Isabella	
Finds land	1492	Columbus	America

Form 3- Paper Fold Skill

Element	Number	Use	Dangers	Future

Form 4- Paper Fold Skill for Science

Chapter 5
LEARNING TO READ

STEPS THAT LEAD TO SUCCESS IN READING:

- Starts with copying a respect for books
- Seeing the written word when being read to
- Identifying pictures and building an oral vocabulary
- Reciting poems
- Learning a story by memory and then reading by sight. This creates a form and vision of a verbal sound. *Example*: "Once" as opposed to "fall", they do not look alike or sound alike.
- A Dolch list of words contains two hundred twenty words, that when learned, can help a child read 66% of

the words in most children's books. Many teacher supplies stores, will have materials containing these words, especially as flash cards

- Phonics – To read words by sounds a child must learn the sounds of consonants and vowels. Consonants are given sounds when combined with vowels. Vowels have sounds when they stand alone. Vowels are a, e, i, o, u and sometimes y.

- Long vowels say their name as in make, be, line, both, cute, and my, y sounds like i. Short vowels have the sounds, a as in apple, e as in egg, i as in it, o as in ox, and u as in up.

In order to help some children master phonetic sounds, the following rhythmic piece may help.

*A is for apple, and a says a, put it in with b
and b says ba   as in bat
A is for apple and a says a put it with c and c
says ca   as in cap
A is for apple and a says a put with d and d
says da   as in dad*

Continue combining consonants with short vowels using some of the following words:
Fat, gap, had, jack, lap, mat, nap, quack, rat, sad, tag, van, wag, yak and zag

E is for elephant as in bed, den, fed, get, hen, jet, keg, let, men, net, pen, quest, red, set, ten, vent, well, yell, zen

I is for Indian as in bin, dip, fit, give, him, jig, kit, lick, mix, nip, pin, quick, rip, sit, tip, vim, win, yip, zip

O is for octopus as in box, cot, doll, fox, got, hot, job, lock, mom, not, pop, rot, sock, top

U is for umbrella as in but, cup, duck, fun, gum, hug, jump, luck, mug, nut, pup, run, sun, tug

You can use this preceding exercise with all the other vowel sounds. Searches with the dictionary may be fun to do to complete lists using all phonics sounds.

You have been given the short vowel sounds with words. Long vowel sound examples are:

ā as in bake

ē as in keep

ī as in ice

ō as in coat

ū as in unite

ÿ as in sky

If you look in the front of the pages of most dictionaries, you will see explanations of all the vowel sounds. It is a good way to make sure you are pronouncing a word correctly.

COMPREHENSION – Understanding what you read

- This skill begins by being able to understand a single word. It helps if a child can use a dictionary and thesaurus

- Next, one has to understand a sentence. Since almost every sentence has a verb, a sentence may answer words such as who, what and where. *Example*:

Jack and Jill went up the hill.

Verb:	went
Question:	who went
Question:	who went where

MAIN IDEA

- To begin finding main idea, one will usually begin by finding the main idea in a paragraph. Most good writers will either have the main idea in the first sentence or the last sentence in a paragraph.

- Another main idea question may be to pick the best title for a group of paragraphs. A good way to pick a title is to find the main idea in each paragraph and use that information to help select the best title.

LOCATING AN ANSWER

- The best way to locate an answer is to read the question first
- The second best way is as you read a passage, underline details such as dates, numbers, colors, size, proper names, places, and/or specific words you think are important. This will help to quickly find an answer

FOLLOWING DIRECTIONS

For this skill it is very important to use diagrams and pictures. Make sure you understand the vocabulary being used

- Sequencing – placing things in order is a very important skill for following directions. Things can be in order by words like first, next and last. Sometimes little to big, old to new, from top to bottom, etc. Learn these words and be sure to understand their use.

MAP READING

Become familiar with north, east, south and west. Latitude, longitude, vertical and horizontal (left to right) will be helpful for map reading

DRAWING CONCLUSIONS

Sometimes skimming a passage and thoroughly reading the questions first, and then reading the passage carefully will help to draw a correct conclusion.

Author's purpose

Is a reading passage meant to be funny, sad, contradictory, or sarcastic? Is the passage meant to sway an opinion or a scare tactic? Think about other purposes an author may have. Do we read a text book in the same way we read a novel?

Vocabulary

- Get a good dictionary
- Get a thesaurus
- Use the glossaries in the back of children's textbooks
- Have family games for who can use the most new words
- Make up crossword puzzles using new words
- Illustrate words

- Use new words in sentences
- Find synonyms for new words
- Post a vocabulary list for the week

GRAMMAR

In addition to reading comprehension, an understanding of grammar helps one develop a strong foundation in the study of English.

I. There are four kinds of sentences

- A **DECLARATIVE SENTENCE** makes a statement and ends with a period
- An **IMPERATIVE SENTENCE** is a command or request and ends with a period
- An **INTERROGATIVE SENTENCE** asks a question and ends with a question mark (?)
- An **EXCLAMATORY SENTENCE** may show excitement, fear, happiness or surprise and end with an exclamation point (!)

II. SHORT REVIEW OF PARTS OF SPEECH

A sentence has a subject and a predicate. The subject tells who or what a sentence is about. The predicate tells what the subject does or is.

NOUNS

Nouns appear in the subject, verbs appear in the predicate. In some sentences, the noun does not appear but it is understood. The verb always appears, except when an author takes poetic license. Example: Go! That is a sentence, whoever you want to go is understood.

COMMON NOUNS

Common nouns name a person, place or thing. Proper nouns name a specific person (Aunt Mame), place (Washington,

DC), thing (Apple iPod). Proper nouns are always capitalized. Plural nouns can be tricky. Just putting an (s) on the end of a word doesn't always make it plural. Some easy differences will show you why to check plurals with a dictionary: singular deer/plural deer; singular knife/plural knives; singular feet/plural foot. Nouns that were once verbs, become gerunds by adding "ing" to them. Some gerunds are: smoking, dancing, playing etc.

ADJECTIVES

Adjectives tell something about nouns. An adjective can describe a noun by color, number, size, specifics; such as this or that. Adjectives can compare by endings of er or est.

Example: *Texas is larger than New Jersey. Brazil is the largest country in South America.*

VERBS

Verbs show action; words such as hop, drive, climb, eat, etc. Verbs also show a state of being; be, is, are, were, etc. The verbs that do not show action but connect, or link to a word in the predicate are called linking verbs. Forms of the verb "be" are common linking verbs Example: Jack was excited to win the prize.

Verbs have tense. If a student is to go on to study a foreign language, understanding about tense in the English language will be very helpful. It also helps with comprehension, sequencing and following directions.

The six tenses you need to be aware of:

1. Present tense

   I dance very often

2. Past tense

   I danced yesterday

3. Future tense

   I will dance tomorrow

4. Present perfect tense

   I have danced many times

5. Past perfect tense

   I had danced before Queen Elizabeth arrived

6. Future perfect tense

   I will have danced for Queen Elizabeth for the next five years

ADVERBS

Adverbs can describe a verb, another adverb and an adjective. Adverbs give information for where, when, how often, how much, how long and in what way. Many adverbs are formed by adding ly to an adjective. "Well" and "good" present problems so choose "well" an adverb to help a verb, and "good" an adjective to help a noun.

Articles

Articles are "a", "an" and "the". They are used as an adjective before a single word. If a word begins with a vowel use "an". Use "a" before a word that begins with a consonant. "The" is used before singular or plural words that begin with vowels or consonants.

Prepositions

Prepositions show direction and place. The following words are prepositions: about, above, along, behind, beneath, beside, by, down, from, in, inside, into, of, on, through, up, with. You may find more, this is just a start. A prepositional phrase is a preposition plus a noun phrase such as: about my room, beneath the stars, with a burst …

SPLIT INFINITIVES

An infinitive is a verb with the word "to" in front of it. When you split an infinitive you are putting words between "to" and the verb. It is usually better not to split the infinitive.

Example: *It is better "to laugh joyously" – sounds better than "to joyously laugh."*

III. PUNCTUATION

Punctuation helps to separate thoughts for better understanding. It brings more structure to written work.

PERIODS

The period tells us that an idea has ended and a new one will begin.

COMMA (,)

The comma tells us to pause and take a breath. A comma has to be in the right place.

Example: *"Mary Jane and Allison went to Andrew's party"*

This sentence is different than: *Mary, Jane and Allison went to Andrew's party.* Reread sentences and make sure they say what you mean – with the help of a comma.

More examples for the use of commas are:

- Between the day and year
  May 20, 2022
- Between the month and year
  May, 2022
- Between a city and state
  Trenton, NJ
- After introductory words
- To set off appositives (appositives

give more information about a word or a phrase)

Example of an appositive: *Jane, the pretty girl in blue, is my new friend.*

- Two adjectives modifying the same noun

  Example: *The large, red cart was full of flowers.*

CONJUNCTIONS

Conjunctions are the enemies of commas. Conjunctions join words or groups of words. Trouble conjunctions are "and" and 'but". Other conjunctions used often are because, for, or, so and yet. Don't use a comma every time you see a conjunction. Some linking conjunctions are whenever, since, while, and when; those conjunctions seldom need commas.

USE OF PUNCTUATION

- Use a comma after conjunctive adverbs. Some conjunctive adverbs are: finally, furthermore, however, therefore.

   Example: *I ran all the way to the station; however, I missed the train.*

- Use a comma after clauses and introductory phrases.

   Example: *Since our last meeting was so successful, I thought we should meet again.*

- Use commas in lists
- Use commas in a direct address
- Use commas in quotations. Commas and periods always go inside the quotation mark.

COLONS

Use colons to introduce lists

- More uses are:
- Between the hour and minutes

- To introduce a long quotation
- After a greeting in a business letter
- When you use phrases: such as, the following, these things
- Between volume and page, or chapter and verse
- For subtitles of books, articles, chapters
- For ratios
- To indicate characters speaking in a play

SEMI-COLONS

Use a semi-colon between two sentences that are closely related

Example: *My house is on Elm Street; your house is on Elm Street.*

Semicolons are used before conjunctive adverbs. Some conjunctive adverbs are: also, besides, certainly, consequently, in fact, in addition, nevertheless.

Sometimes it is good to use semicolons when a sentence has a lot of commas

APOSTROPHES

Use apostrophes:

- in contractions – do not, don't
- In possessive nouns – Bob's house
- In plurals of letters or words: John got five B's

HYPHENS

Use hyphens:

- Between syllables at the end of a line
- Use hyphens with some prefixes, like: ex-husband, great-uncle, co-author
- Use hyphens with some compound words: president-elect, self-motivator
- Use hyphens when a word would be confusing or hard to read
  Example: *Jack removed his jacket as he was ready to re-move the furniture to a new set-*

ting

- Use a hyphen with double last names
- Use a hyphen with compound numbers from 21-99
  Example: *twenty-one, one hundred ninety-nine*
- Use a hyphen with compound adjectives if they appear before the noun
  Example: *the six-year-old child, the tenth-grade student*

PARENTHESES

- Use as an explanation
  Example: *The new girl (the one who moved from California), won the highest academic award.*
- Use for a translation.
  Example: *Imagine someone in this age, using LOL (laughing out loud) who doesn't text message.*
- When punctuating with parentheses,

the comma goes outside. The period goes outside too; unless, the parentheses envelop a complete sentence.

- You can use an exclamation point (!) inside a parenthetical comment that is exclamatory.
Example: *We love the birthday cake (it's scrumptious!).*
- If only the parenthetical comment is a question, the question mark goes inside the parentheses. If the whole sentence is a question, the question mark goes outside.

ELIPSES

Elpises are used to replace left out words. The most common use of elipses that I have seen are usually long quotations. An author starts the quote, gets his/her point across and ends with elipses.

EXCLAMATION POINTS

Use exclamation marks after strong remarks. Wow! Oh my! There is a fire! What an amazing ride! We won!

Chapter 6
Math Skills

Using numbers can begin at birth.
Count objects whenever you can. It is
important to show the relationship of
numbers to objects. Putting objects
out in groups of one and two and three;
children will soon realize that one is less
than two and three is more than two.
If your children can count to ten or
more before entering kindergarten, math
in school will be fun. Familiarity with
circles, squares, triangles and rectangles
may also make beginning math less of a
challenge.

For addition and subtraction, children
can use fingers and toes. They can also
use a number line. I like giving them

a tongue depressor and putting twenty dots on it with numbers below.

.	.	.	.	.	.	.	.	.	.	.	.	.	.	.	.	.	.	.	.
1	2	3	4	5	6	7	8	9	10	11	12	13	14	15	16	17	18	19	20

Hopefully, as they add and subtract enough times, it will be quicker to use their brain than a calculator.

Multiplication and division will be more difficult for some children. I like to use learning styles as a jumping point. Some children learn easily by rote. Flash cards will work well for those children.

Some children learn best by auditory pre- sentations. They really need to hear the multiplication tables. For those students I have written a song, or rap, simply called "The Multiplication Song". A copy of the words can be found on page 82.

Some children learn best by visualizing. For those students, a special sheet allows them to see that "Products Make Patterns." The sheet has the children color in the answers to the multiplication tables. If an answer is wrong, the pattern looks wrong. Answers to multiplication facts are called products, see pages 84-93.

Then we have the very active children who need their whole body involved. Most times I think this activity is for all students.

An obstacle course is planned with ten stations. Each station has a different activity

- Hopping
- Jumping
- Bouncing ball
- Jumping over a line
- Hopping over a line
- Throwing a ball up and catching it with both hands
- Throwing a ball up and catching with one hand
- Marching
- Throwing a ball up, clapping and catching
- Clapping and marching

At each station they have to count by that number to 10 times the number. Example: station 4 – 4, 8, 12, 16, 20, 24, 28, 32, 36, 40, Each person playing gets an index card with their name on it. As they complete a station successfully, the person in charge of that station initials the card with the station number and their initials. Example station 4 – MF. This can be played at home and at school.

Some help with division, especially long division, is to use graph paper. When every number has a home it is easier to do. For example: 679235 divided by 385:

						1	7	6	4
385			6	7	9	2	3	5
			3	8	5			
			2	9	4	2		
			2	6	9	5		
				2	4	7	3	
				2	3	1	0	
					1	6	3	5
					1	5	4	0
							9	5

Fractions need to be seen for most students. If you have a pie, cut it into many equal pieces. Make sure your child understands the bottom number (denominator) states how many cuts were made equally in the whole pie. The number on top (numerator) tells how many pieces you will use.

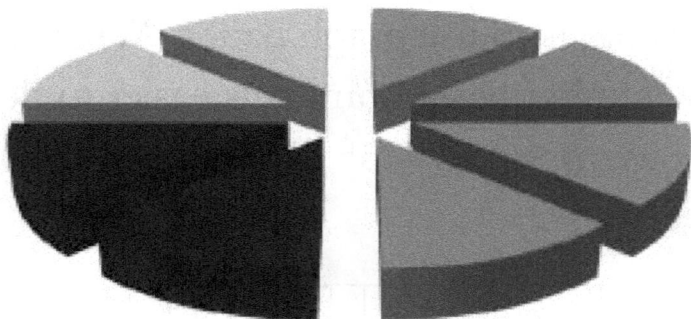

$\frac{2}{8}$ *dark gray*

$\frac{4}{8}$ *medium gray*

$\frac{2}{8}$ *light gray*

When **ADDING OR SUBTRACTING FRACTIONS,** they have to have the same denominators.

$$\begin{array}{r} \frac{1}{2} = \frac{2}{4} \\ + \ \frac{1}{4} = \frac{1}{4} \\ \hline \frac{3}{4} = \frac{3}{4} \end{array}$$

Every time you have a numerator and denominator that is equal, you have a whole number.

$$\frac{5}{5} = 1 \qquad \frac{3}{5} + \frac{2}{5} = \frac{5}{5} = 1$$

A whole number and a fraction is called a **MIXED NUMBER.**

$$2\frac{1}{4}$$

MULTIPLICATION OF FRACTIONS

$$\frac{1}{4} \times \frac{1}{4} = \frac{1}{16}$$

To multiply a mixed number by a fraction, change the mixed number to a fraction.

$$5\frac{1}{4} \times \frac{3}{8}$$

- Change 5¼ to a fraction by multiplying the denominator (4) by the whole number(5) and adding the numerator (1). Then place your answer over the denominator:

$$\frac{4 \times 5 + 1}{4} = \frac{21}{4}$$

- Now multiply:

$$\frac{21}{4} \times \frac{3}{8} = \frac{63}{32}$$

- Change your answer 63/32 to a mixed number by dividing the numerator (63) by the denominator (32):

$$
1\frac{31}{32}
$$

$$
32\overline{)63}
$$

$$
\underline{32}
$$

$$
31
$$

- Final answer:

$$5\frac{1}{4} \times \frac{3}{8} = 1\frac{31}{32}$$

DIVISION OF FRACTIONS

To divide fractions, simply turn divisor upside down and multiply.

$$\frac{1}{3} \div \frac{1}{4} \text{ becomes } \frac{1}{3} \times \frac{4}{1} = \frac{4}{3} = 1\frac{1}{3}$$

$$5\frac{1}{4} \div \frac{3}{4} \text{ becomes } \frac{21}{4} \times \frac{4}{3} = \frac{84}{12} = 7$$

DECIMALS

.1 reads 1/10   *one tenth*
.01 reads 1/100   *one one hundredth*
.001 reads 1/1000   *one one thousandth*

55.04 reads 55 and four one hundredths.

Adding decimals keep decimal point in same position, subtraction the same.

```
    8.1          6.04
   16.3         -3.51
  342.56         2.53
  366.96
```

MULTIPLICATION OF DECIMALS

Count decimal places and place decimal point that many places from the right.

$$
\begin{array}{r}
5.62 \\
.304 \\
\hline
2248 \\
1\,686 \\
\hline
1.70848
\end{array}
$$

DIVISION OF DECIMALS

Make the divisor a whole number by moving the decimal point to the right. Then move the same number of places in the dividend.

$$
\begin{array}{r}
2.5 \quad \textit{quotient} \\
2.5\overline{)6.25} \quad \textit{dividend} \\
\textit{divisor} \quad 5\,0 \\
\hline
1\,25 \\
1\,25 \\
\hline
0
\end{array}
$$

PERCENT

Percent is a part of 100

$$\frac{1}{100} = 1\%$$

$$\frac{10}{100} = 10\%$$

$$\frac{100}{100} = 100\%$$

These math skills, as presented, should give you confidence to learn more.

One of the best books I recommend for understanding math in the upper grades is "Cliffs Math Review for Standardized Tests".

Attachment 1 - Counting Rhyme

Here we are in a line
Pointing toes and feeling fine
First one points
Next one too
$1 + 1 = 2$

First two point
Next two more
$2 + 2 = 4$

First three point
Three stay fixed
$3 + 3 = 6$

First four point
Then four to mate
$4 + 4 = 8$

Five will point
Then five again
$5 + 5 = 10$

Attachment 2 - Counting Rhyme

Multiplication Song
© Marcia Friedman

Whenever you multiply by one, the answer is the same.
As the number multiplied, you answer we'll have a game
1x1 ___, 1x2 ___, 1x3 ___, you see; it's easy as A, B, C.
1x4 ___, 1x5 ___, 1x6 ___, you know; now up the line we go.
1x7 ___, 1x8 ___, 1x9 ___, my friends: and so our table ends.

Instead of adding one plus one, let's multiply by two.
All your answers will be even, show what you can do.
2x1 ___, 2x2 ___, 2x3 ___, you see; it's easy as A, B, C.
2x4 ___, 2x5 ___, 2x6 ___, you know; now up the line we go.
2x7 ___, 2x8 ___, 2x9 ___, my friends: and so our table ends.

When we multiply by three, it triples numbers quickly.
It saves us lots and lots of time; let's multiply by three.
3x1 ___, 3x2 ___, 3x3 ___, you see; it's easy as A, B, C.
3x4 ___, 3x5 ___, 3x6 ___, you know; now up the line we go.
3x7 ___, 3x8 ___, 3x9 ___, my friends: and so our table ends.

If we add the same number, four times in a row,
You will see that same number grow, and grow, and grow.
and grow.
4x1 ___, 4x2 ___, 4x3 ___, you see; it's easy as A, B, C.
4x4 ___, 4x5 ___, 4x6 ___, you know; now up the line we go.
4x7 ___, 4x8 ___, 4x9 ___, my friends: and so our table ends.

Fives and zeroes only, that's all that it can be.
If your answer's something else, you're wrong as you can
see.
5x1 ___, 5x2 ___, 5x3 ___, you see; it's easy as A, B, C.
5x4 ___, 5x5 ___, 5x6 ___, you know; now up the line we go.
5x7 ___, 5x8 ___, 5x9 ___, my friends: and so our table ends.

The sixes are the table, that we will do right now.
I hope that you are able, then you can take a bow.
6x1 ___, 6x2 ___, 6x3 ___, you see; it's easy as A, B, C.
6x4 ___, 6x5 ___, 6x6 ___, you know; now up the line we go.
6x7 ___, 6x8 ___, 6x9 ___, my friends: and so our table ends.

When you're ready for seven, you're really on your way.
So concentrate and take your time, I'm sure you'll do just fine.
7x1 ___, 7x2 ___, 7x3 ___, you see; it's easy as A, B, C.
7x4 ___, 7x5 ___, 7x6 ___, you know; now up the line we go.
7x7 ___, 7x8 ___, 7x9 ___, my friends: and so our table ends.

Eights are really nothing more, than combinations of two times four.
All even numbers there will be, so let's do eights and you will see.
8x1 ___, 8x2 ___, 8x3 ___, you see; it's easy as A, B, C.
8x4 ___, 8x5 ___, 8x6 ___, you know; now up the line we go.
8x7 ___, 8x8 ___, 8x9 ___, my friends: and so our table ends.

The last table we will do, nines for me and nines for you.
Add the answers you will find, every one will equal nine.
9x1 ___, 9x2 ___, 9x3 ___, you see; it's easy as A, B, C.
9x4 ___, 9x5 ___, 9x6 ___, you know; now up the line we go.
9x7 ___, 9x8 ___, 9x9 ___, my friends: and so our table ends.

Products Make Patterns

©Marcia Friedman

Quickly see multiplication table results and the patterns that the correct answers make.

1	2	3	4	5	6	7	8	9	10

1	2	3	4	5	6	7	8	9	10

The following pages will show you the patterns that result from multiplication. Each page will represent a number.

Multiply by 2

1	2	3	4	5	6	7	8	9	10
11	12	13	14	15	16	17	18	19	20

1	2	3	4	5	6	7	8	9	10
11	12	13	14	15	16	17	18	19	20

PRODUCTS MAKE PATTERNS

©Marcia Friedman

Multiply by 3

1	2	3	4	5	6	7	8	9	10
11	12	13	14	15	16	17	18	19	20
21	22	23	24	25	26	27	28	29	30

1	2	3	4	5	6	7	8	9	10
11	12	13	14	15	16	17	18	19	20
21	22	23	24	25	26	27	28	29	30

PRODUCTS MAKE PATTERNS

©Marcia Friedman

Multiply by 4

1	2	3	4	5	6	7	8	9	10
11	12	13	14	15	16	17	18	19	20
21	22	23	24	25	26	27	28	29	30
31	32	33	34	35	36	37	38	39	40

1	2	3	4	5	6	7	8	9	10
11	12	13	14	15	16	17	18	19	20
21	22	23	24	25	26	27	28	29	30
31	32	33	34	35	36	37	38	39	40

PRODUCTS MAKE PATTERNS

©Marcia Friedman

Multiply by 5

1	2	3	4	5	6	7	8	9	10
11	12	13	14	15	16	17	18	19	20
21	22	23	24	25	26	27	28	29	30
31	32	33	34	35	36	37	38	39	40
41	42	43	44	45	46	47	48	49	50

1	2	3	4	5	6	7	8	9	10
11	12	13	14	15	16	17	18	19	20
21	22	23	24	25	26	27	28	29	30
31	32	33	34	35	36	37	38	39	40
41	42	43	44	45	46	47	48	49	50

PRODUCTS MAKE PATTERNS

©Marcia Friedman

Multiply by 6

1	2	3	4	5	6	7	8	9	10
11	12	13	14	15	16	17	18	19	20
21	22	23	24	25	26	27	28	29	30
31	32	33	34	35	36	37	38	39	40
41	42	43	44	45	46	47	48	49	50
51	52	53	54	55	56	57	58	59	60

1	2	3	4	5	6	7	8	9	10
11	12	13	14	15	16	17	18	19	20
21	22	23	24	25	26	27	28	29	30
31	32	33	34	35	36	37	38	39	40
41	42	43	44	45	46	47	48	49	50
51	52	53	54	55	56	57	58	59	60

PRODUCTS MAKE PATTERNS

©Marcia Friedman

Multiply by 7

1	2	3	4	5	6	7	8	9	10
11	12	13	14	15	16	17	18	19	20
21	22	23	24	25	26	27	28	29	30
31	32	33	34	35	36	37	38	39	40
41	42	43	44	45	46	47	48	49	50
51	52	53	54	55	56	57	58	59	60
61	62	63	64	65	66	67	68	69	70

1	2	3	4	5	6	7	8	9	10
11	12	13	14	15	16	17	18	19	20
21	22	23	24	25	26	27	28	29	30
31	32	33	34	35	36	37	38	39	40
41	42	43	44	45	46	47	48	49	50
51	52	53	54	55	56	57	58	59	60
61	62	63	64	65	66	67	68	69	70

PRODUCTS MAKE PATTERNS

©Marcia Friedman

Multiply by 8

1	2	3	4	5	6	7	8	9	10
11	12	13	14	15	16	17	18	19	20
21	22	23	24	25	26	27	28	29	30
31	32	33	34	35	36	37	38	39	40
41	42	43	44	45	46	47	48	49	50
51	52	53	54	55	56	57	58	59	60
61	62	63	64	65	66	67	68	69	70
71	72	73	74	75	76	77	78	79	80

1	2	3	4	5	6	7	8	9	10
11	12	13	14	15	16	17	18	19	20
21	22	23	24	25	26	27	28	29	30
31	32	33	34	35	36	37	38	39	40
41	42	43	44	45	46	47	48	49	50
51	52	53	54	55	56	57	58	59	60
61	62	63	64	65	66	67	68	69	70
71	72	73	74	75	76	77	78	79	80

PRODUCTS MAKE PATTERNS

©Marcia Friedman

Multiply by 9

1	2	3	4	5	6	7	8	9	10
11	12	13	14	15	16	17	18	19	20
21	22	23	24	25	26	27	28	29	30
31	32	33	34	35	36	37	38	39	40
41	42	43	44	45	46	47	48	49	50
51	52	53	54	55	56	57	58	59	60
61	62	63	64	65	66	67	68	69	70
71	72	73	74	75	76	77	78	79	80
81	82	83	84	85	86	87	88	89	90

1	2	3	4	5	6	7	8	9	10
11	12	13	14	15	16	17	18	19	20
21	22	23	24	25	26	27	28	29	30
31	32	33	34	35	36	37	38	39	40
41	42	43	44	45	46	47	48	49	50
51	52	53	54	55	56	57	58	59	60
61	62	63	64	65	66	67	68	69	70
71	72	73	74	75	76	77	78	79	80
81	82	83	84	85	86	87	88	89	90

PRODUCTS MAKE PATTERNS

©Marcia Friedman

Multiply by 10

1	2	3	4	5	6	7	8	9	10
11	12	13	14	15	16	17	18	19	20
21	22	23	24	25	26	27	28	29	30
31	32	33	34	35	36	37	38	39	40
41	42	43	44	45	46	47	48	49	50
51	52	53	54	55	56	57	58	59	60
61	62	63	64	65	66	67	68	69	70
71	72	73	74	75	76	77	78	79	80
81	82	83	84	85	86	87	88	89	90
91	92	93	94	95	96	97	98	99	100

1	2	3	4	5	6	7	8	9	10
11	12	13	14	15	16	17	18	19	20
21	22	23	24	25	26	27	28	29	30
31	32	33	34	35	36	37	38	39	40
41	42	43	44	45	46	47	48	49	50
51	52	53	54	55	56	57	58	59	60
61	62	63	64	65	66	67	68	69	70
71	72	73	74	75	76	77	78	79	80
81	82	83	84	85	86	87	88	89	90
91	92	93	94	95	96	97	98	99	100

PRODUCTS MAKE PATTERNS

©Marcia Friedman

Chapter 7

Science

Try to make science fun by talking about the different concepts that make up the study of science. Do easy experiments that help explain the different areas that make up a science program?

In some homes, children become more interested in science through association with the animal world. Many have pets and parents can find lots of information about a pet to share with their child. Visits to zoos and local petting farms are fun. Reading books about animals widens childrens' scope of knowledge. My daughter listened to a story about a horse named Sunflower. She wanted a horse that she could name Sunflower – well a horse was not affordable, but a puppy was. So we ended up with a dog named Sunflower.

Plants are another good way to create an interest in science. Plant a garden in the yard or place seeds on sponges and watch them grow. Make a scrapbook with pictures of flowers in alphabetical order.

A bird feeder is another way to get children excited about science.

When they start to study science in school, discuss it with them. Show them how interesting you think it is and try to think of ways science is used in our everyday lives. If the school has a science fair, make your child believe that participation in the science fair is just as important as participation in sports or music or art.

Just how math is divided into different areas, such as addition, subtraction, multiplication, division, fractions, percents, algebra, geometry and so on; science also has its parts. To name some parts, there are:

- **PHYSICS**, which deals with motion force, energy;
- **CHEMISTRY**, the study of composition, properties of odd and notable parts of elementary substances;
- **BIOLOGY**, the study of living organisms;
- **SPACE**, the study of the solar system and the space program;
- **ANATOMY**, the study of the body.

A few more ideas about equipment to make learning science easier:

- **PHYSICS** – balls, ropes, wood slats, thermometers
- **CHEMISTRY** – baking supplies, small metal pieces, a large chart showing the elements
- **BIOLOGY** – pictures of plants, animals, birds, fish, seeds, sponges
- **ANATOMY** – a large paper skeleton
- **SPACE** – pictures of astronauts and space vehicles, drawings of the solar system

Element	Number	Use	Dangers	Future

Form 5 - Pleated Paper Preparer

Chapter 8
Social Studies

Social studies can be a combination of history and geography. Some schools teach them separately at different grade levels and some combine the two areas into one.

Read the Tables of Contents of your child's textbook, and you will know what they will be studying. In the chapter on Homework, I suggested some materials and ideas about making social studies come alive. You may want to go back and take a second look.

When studying for a test in social studies, I would suggest the "pleated paper preparer".

Form 5 - Pleated Paper Preparer

Happenings	Dates	People	Place
Wants to find new lands	1490s	Columbus	Spain
Asks for financial help		Queen Isabella	
Finds land	1492	Columbus	America

After the info has been filled in, someone can say one of the words on the line and the student tries to fill in the rest of the information. If studying alone, make two copies – one all filled in and another with only one word on a line filled in. The idea is to try and fill in all of the missing information.

Another good idea is to make sure the student reads all of the lead statements or rubric and can summarize what it means.

Maps and locations can be tricky. I remember in Grade 4 I had to locate England. I knew the map showed New Jersey on the eastern side of the United States. The map of Europe was below and England was east of New Jersey, so I said England was in the eastern part of

Europe. Make sure you have a map of the world.

I didn't match up the Atlantic Ocean. I have never forgotten that mistake. It cost me my first paper without a 100%.

Chapter 9
Understand Test Scores, Grading and Report Cards

Standardized test scores are adopted by the companies that produce them. Sometimes they are
Grade levels and sometimes percentiles. Grade levels could be represented by 5.1 – fifth grade 1st month, or it may be 75th percentile, which means the student did better than 75% of the students taking that test. If the percentiles are only for the community taking the test and most students are working below grade level, the percentile is not what a person parenting for school success wants. If percentiles are for state levels, US levels or foreign countries; this would be very

helpful for comparisons. The grade level would be a better way to know if your child is achieving success.

Grading for teacher structured tests should be explained by the teacher as there may be different ways of grading for different types of materials.

Report card grading will also have to be explained by the teacher before reports are distributed. When a parent understands the report card, they are better able to discuss the report with their child.

Parent Reference Books

Ames, Louise Bates., Frances L. Ilg, Carol Chase. Haber, and Betty David. **YOUR ONE-YEAR-OLD: 12 TO 24 MONTHS, FUN-LOVING AND FUSSY.** New York, NY: Dell, 1983. Print.

Ames, Louise Bates., and Frances L. Ilg. **YOUR TWO-YEAR-OLD: TERRIBLE OR TENDER.** New York, NY: Dell, 1980. Print.

Ames, Louise Bates., and Frances L. Ilg. **YOUR THREE YEAR OLD.** Loughton: Piatkus, 1983. Print.

Ames, Louise Bates., and Frances L. Ilg. **YOUR FOUR-YEAR-OLD: WILD AND WONDERFUL.** New York: Delacorte, 1976. Print.

Ames, Louise Bates., and Frances L. Ilg. **YOUR FIVE-YEAR-OLD: SUNNY AND SE-RENE.** New York, NY: Dell Pub., 1981. Print.

Ames, Louise Bates., and Frances L. Ilg. **YOUR SIX-YEAR-OLD: LOVING AND DEFI-ANT.** New York: Dell, 1981. Print.

Ames, Louise Bates., and Carol Chase. Haber. **YOUR SEVEN-YEAR-OLD: LIFE IN A MINOR KEY.** New York: Delacorte, 1985. Print.

Ames, Louise Bates., and Carol Chase. Haber. **YOUR EIGHT-YEAR-OLD: LIVELY AND OUTGOING.** New York, NY: Delacorte, 1989. Print.

Ames, Louise Bates., and Carol Chase. Haber. **YOUR NINE-YEAR-OLD: THOUGHTFUL AND MYSTERIOUS.** New York, NY: Dell Trade Paperback, 1991. Print.

Ames, Louise B. **YOUR TEN TO FOURTEEN YEAR OLD.** [S.l.]: Delacorte, 1989. Print.

Baron, Bruce, Christine Baron, and Bonnie MacDonald. **WHAT DID YOU LEARN IN SCHOOL TODAY?: A COMPREHENSIVE GUIDE TO GETTING THE BEST POSSIBLE EDUCATION FOR YOUR CHILDREN.** New York, NY: Warner, 1983. Print.

Bell, Terrel H. **ACTIVE PARENT CONCERN:
A NEW HOME GUIDE TO HELP YOUR
CHILD DO BETTER IN SCHOOL.** Engle-
wood Cliffs, NJ: Prentice-Hall, 1976.
Print.

Bobrow, Jerry. **MATH REVIEW FOR STAN-
DARDIZED TESTS.** Chichester: John Wiley
& Sons, 2010. Print.

Cheatum, Billye Ann., and Allison **A.
HAMMOND. PHYSICAL ACTIVITIES FOR
IMPROVING CHILDREN'S LEARNING AND
BEHAVIOR: A GUIDE TO SENSORY MOTOR
DEVELOPMENT.** Champaign, IL: Human
Kinetics, 2000. Print.

Covino, William A., and Peter Z. Orton.
**CLIFFS VERBAL REVIEW FOR STANDARD-
IZED TESTS.** Lincoln, Neb.: Cliffs Notes,
1986. Print.

Fromboluti, Carol Sue. **HELPING YOUR CHILD LEARN GEOGRAPHY.** [Washington, D.C.]: U.S. Dept. of Education, Office of Educational Research and Improvement, 1990. Print.

Ginott, Haim G. **TEACHER AND CHILD; A BOOK FOR PARENTS AND TEACHERS.** New York: Macmillan, 1972. Print.

Gruber, Gary R. **DR. GRUBER'S ESSENTIAL GUIDE TO TEST TAKING FOR KIDS.** New York: Quill, 1986. Print.

Kutner, Lawrence. **PARENT & CHILD: GETTING THROUGH TO EACH OTHER.** New York: Avon, 1992. Print.

Louv, Richard. **CHILDHOOD'S FUTURE.** New York: Anchor, 1992. Print.

Perkinson, Kathryn. **HELPING YOUR CHILD LEARN GEOGRAPHY: WITH ACTIVITIES FOR CHILDREN FROM 5 TO 10 YEARS OF AGE**. [Washington, D.C.]: U.S. Dept. of Education, Office of Educational Research and Improvement in Cooperation with U.S. Dept. of the Interior, U.S. Geological Survey & National Geographic Society, 1996. Print.

Schwartz, Eugene M. **HOW TO DOUBLE YOUR CHILD'S GRADES IN SCHOOL: BUILD BRILLIANCE AND LEADERSHIP INTO YOUR CHILD--FROM KINDERGARTEN TO COLLEGE--IN JUST 5 MINUTES A DAY**. New York: Barnes & Noble, 1999. Print.

Seligman, Martin E. P. **LEARNED OPTI-MISM: HOW TO CHANGE YOUR MIND AND YOUR LIFE.** New York: Vintage, 2006. Print.

Trelease, Jim. **THE READ-ALOUD HANDBOOK.** New York: Penguin, 2006. Print.

VanCleave, Janice Pratt. **JANICE VANCLEAVE'S GUIDE TO MORE OF THE BEST SCIENCE FAIR PROJECTS.** New York: Wiley, 2000. Print.

NURSERY RHYMES & FAIRY TALES, PUZZLES AND GAMES. Carson-Dellosa Publishing Company

Index

A

B

C

D

G

H

I

K

L

M

N

O

P

Q

R

S

T

U

V

W

www.ingramcontent.com/pod-product-compliance
Lightning Source LLC
Chambersburg PA
CBHW071004040426
42443CB00007B/656